Whose Coat Is This?

A Look at How Workers Cover Up— Jackets, Smocks, and Robes

by Laura Purdie Salas
illustrated by Amy Bailey Muehlenhardt

PICTURE WINDOW BOOKS
Minneapolis, Minnesota

Special thanks to our advisers for their expertise:

Rick Levine, Publisher
Made To Measure and Uniform Market News Magazine
Highland Park, Illinois

Susan Kesselring, M.A., Literacy Educator
Rosemount–Apple Valley–Eagan (Minnesota) School District

Editor: Christianne Jones
Designer: Joe Anderson
Page Production: Amy Baily Muehlenhardt, Zach Trover
Editorial Director: Carol Jones
Creative Director: Keith Griffin
The illustrations in this book were prepared digitally.

Picture Window Books
5115 Excelsior Boulevard
Suite 232
Minneapolis, MN 55416
877-845-8392
www.picturewindowbooks.com

Printed in the United States of America.

Library of Congress Cataloging-in-Publication Data
Salas, Laura Purdie.
Whose coat is this? : a look at how workers cover up—jackets, smocks, and robes /
by Laura Purdie Salas ; illustrated by Amy Bailey Muehlenhardt.
p. cm. — (Whose is it?)
Includes bibliographical references and index.
ISBN 1-4048-1598-8 (hardcover)
1. Coats—Juvenile literature. I. Muehlenhardt, Amy Bailey, 1974- ill. II. Title. III. Series.

GT2079.S25 2006
391—dc22   2005021847

Cover up and guess whose coat is whose.

Workers wear many kinds of coats. Some coats keep workers clean, warm, or safe. Other coats are part of a uniform. Coats can be stiff or flowing. They can be heavy or light. They can be clean or spattered.

Not all coats look alike because they are used for different jobs.

Can you tell whose coat is whose?

Look in the back for more information about coats.

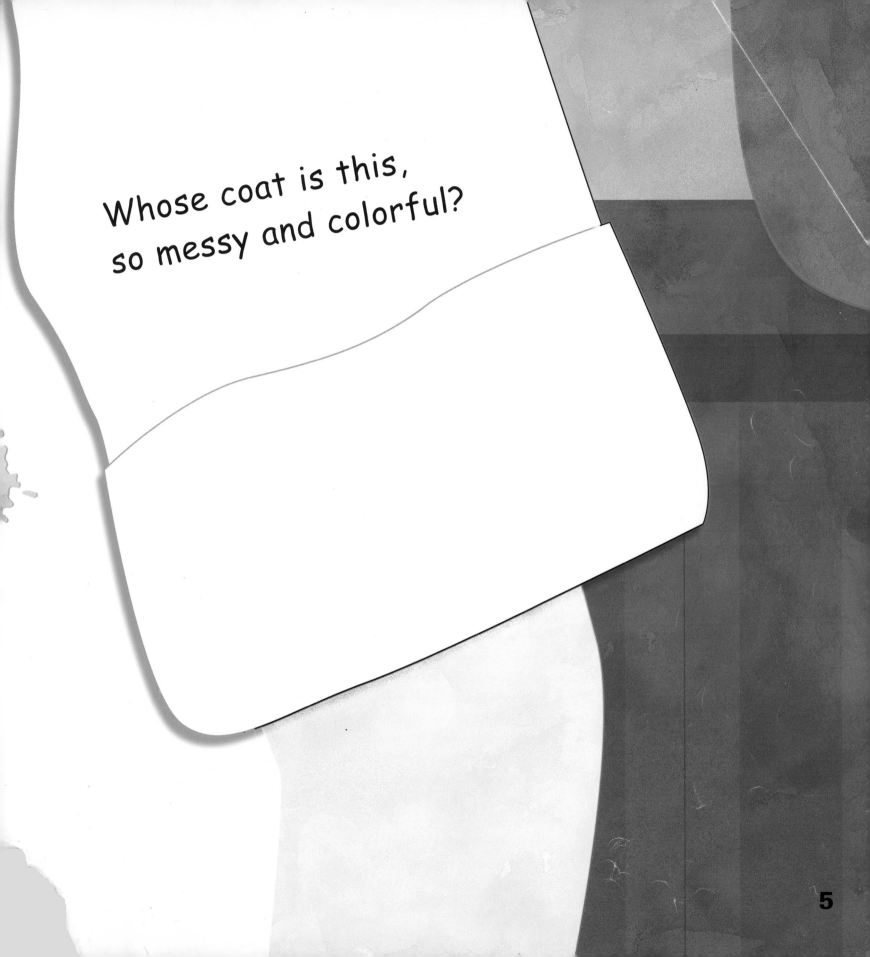

Whose coat is this,
so messy and colorful?

This is an artist's smock.

It keeps his clothes clean. The more an artist works, the messier his smock gets! He puts extra paint brushes in his pocket.

Fun Fact: You might wear a smock, too. When you make messy art projects, it's a good idea to cover your clothes so they stay clean.

6

Whose coat is this,
flowing and black?

This is a judge's robe.

It covers most of her outfit. A judge works in a courtroom. When people don't agree with each other, the judge decides how to solve the problem fairly.

Fun Fact: Judges' robes are based on Roman togas from more than 2,000 years ago.

Whose coat is this, with gold buttons and bars?

This is a soldier's jacket. *Coat*

A soldier wears a uniform to let others know that he is part of a group. The bars show people his rank. Other insignia on the jacket showcase his awards and skills.

Fun Fact: The Army, Navy, Marines, Airforce, and Coast Guard all have special uniforms.

10

Whose coat is this,
waterproof and blue?

This is a mail carrier's coat.

Mail carriers deliver mail to homes and businesses. They deliver mail through all kinds of weather. Their coats are waterproof to keep them dry in wet weather.

Fun Fact: The U.S. Postal Service receives, sorts, and delivers millions of letters, bills, advertisements, and packages every day.

Whose coat is this, so warm and bright?

This is a ski patroller's jacket.

A ski patroller helps people on the ski slopes.
He rescues people who are hurt or stranded.
The coat's bright color makes him easy
to spot.

Fun Fact: The patroller's jacket has
a cross on it. This shape tells skier
and snowboarders that the patrolle
can help them.

Whose coat is this,
so clean and white?

This is a doctor's lab coat.

Does this coat remind you of a scientist? That's because doctors are also scientists. Doctors wear lab coats when they work with patients, chemicals, and medicine.

Fun fact: Many students go through a White Coat Ceremony when they start medical school. During the ceremony, they get their first white coat.

Whose coat is this,
so thick and strong?

17

This is a firefighter's coat.

It has a pocket for a radio so she can talk to other firefighters. It has reflective trim so that other people can see her in dark places. A firefighter's coat is fireproof so the coat will not burn.

Fun Fact: When a firefighter is dressed in all the protective clothes and firefighting equipment needed to fight a fire, she is carrying about 100 pounds (45 kilograms) of gear.

19

This is your coat!

It protects you from the wind and keeps you toasty on cold days. What other kinds of coats do you wear?

Fun Fact: Many animals grow thicker fur coats during the winter.

Just for Fun

Whose coat is whose? Point to the picture
of the coat described in each sentence.

* My bright color helps others see me.

   ski patroller's jacket

* My fireproof fabric keeps me safe.

   firefighter's jacket

* I protect clothes from getting dirty.

   artist's smock

All Kinds of Coats

Duster

Cowboys started wearing long, light coats called dusters in the 1800s. Dusters kept dust and rain off cowboys' clothes and were split up the back. When cowboys rode their horses, half of the duster was on one side of the horse and half was on the other side.

Yellow Rain Slickers

People who fish or work on boats often wear bright yellow rain slickers. The lemon color makes them easy to see. Workers and rescuers can see a yellow slicker more easily in the water than a gray or blue one.

Trench Coat

During World War I (1914-1918), soldiers and officers lived in the trenches. The trenches were cold and wet. The long coats the British army gave to soldiers to help them stay warm and dry became known as trench coats.

Suit Coat

People all over the United States often wear suits to their jobs. The suit coat fits snugly and buttons down the front. Business people usually wear a suit coat with pants or a skirt made out of the same fabric.

Glossary

chemicals—substances made by scientists

fireproof—does not burn

insignia—badges and medals that show someone has certain skills or awards

reflective—to throw back light

soldier—someone who belongs to the military

stranded—left behind

togas—loose robes worn in ancient Rome

trenches—long, narrow ditches

uniforms—special clothes that members of a particular group wear

waterproof—not letting water pass through

To Learn More

At the Library

McNab, Chris. *Everyday Dress.* Broomall, Penn.: Mason Crest, 2003.

Perl, Lila. *From Top Hats to Baseball Caps, From Bustles to Blue Jeans: Why We Dress the Way We Do.* New York: Clarion Books, 1990.

Williams, Barbara. *ABC's of Uniforms and Outfits.* Nashville, Tenn.: Winston-Derek, 1992.

On the Web

FactHound offers a safe, fun way to find Internet sites related to this book. All of the sites on FactHound have been researched by our staff.

1. Visit *www.facthound.com*
2. Type in this special code for age-appropriate sites: 1404815988
3. Click on the Fetch It button.

Your trusty FactHound will fetch the best sites for you!

Index

Look for all of the books in the Whose Is It? series:

Whose Coat Is This?
1-4048-1598-8

Whose Ears Are These?
1-4048-0004-2

Whose Eyes Are These?
1-4048-0005-0

Whose Feet Are These?
1-4048-0006-9

Whose Food Is This?
1-4048-0607-5

Whose Gloves Are These?
1-4048-1599-6

Whose Hat Is This?
1-4048-1600-3

Whose House Is This?
1-4048-0608-3

Whose Legs Are These?
1-4048-0007-7

Whose Mouth Is This?
1-4048-0008-5

Whose Nose Is This?
1-4048-0009-3

Whose Shadow Is This?
1-4048-0609-1

Whose Shoes Are These?
1-4048-1601-1

Whose Skin Is This?
1-4048-0010-7

Whose Sound Is This?
1-4048-0610-5

Whose Spots Are These?
1-4048-0611-3

Whose Tail Is This?
1-4048-0011-5

Whose Tools Are These?
1-4048-1602-X

Whose Vehicle Is This?
1-4048-1603-8

Whose Work Is This?
1-4048-0612-1